/Grammar
Geek

An Hachette UK Company
www.hachette.co.uk

First published in Great Britain in 2019 by Cassell, an imprint of
Octopus Publishing Group Ltd
Carmelite House
50 Victoria Embankment
London EC4Y 0DZ
www.octopusbooks.co.uk

Distributed in the US by Hachette Book Group
1290 Avenue of the Americas
4th and 5th Floors
New York, NY 10104

Distributed in Canada by Canadian Manda Group
664 Annette St., Toronto, Ontario, Canada M6S 2C8

Text by Michael Powell
Design by Milestone Creative

ISBN 978 1 78840 200 2

A CIP catalogue record for this book is available from the
British Library.

Printed and bound in China

10 9 8 7 6 5 4 3 2 1

Introduction

English is full of beauty and surprises, yet, despite being the lingua franca of the globalized world, it has a reputation for being difficult to learn because its grammar has so many quirks and contradictions. This also makes it 'superdope', so it's time to get your geek on!

This book is filled with amuse-bouches about the system and structure of the English language, as well as some useful rules to help you sort out some of those niggling blind spots once and for all. If you've never managed to nail apostrophes or when to use initial capital letters or an ellipsis, the rules are right here, along with common grammar mistakes, often confused words and interesting figures of speech.

Many of us don't even know the basics, so not only does this book reveal some obscure grammar rules and bogus ones you can safely ignore, it's also a mini primer, so in future you'll have no excuse for dangling a modifier or misplacing a semicolon.

Parts of speech

– In English, there are eight parts of speech: <u>noun</u>, <u>pronoun</u>, <u>adjective</u>, <u>verb</u>, <u>adverb</u>, <u>preposition</u>, <u>conjunction</u> and <u>interjection</u>.

Many grammar and spelling rules were made up by a clutch of grumpy white men in England in the eighteenth century, who thought the English language should behave like Latin.
Helen Zaltzman

1 **Nouns**
are naming words.

2 **Pronouns**
replace nouns.

3 **Adjectives**
are describing words.

4 **Verbs**
are doing words.

5 **Adverbs**
tell you how and when.

6 **Prepositions**
are little words (usually)
that tell you where and
when.

7 **Conjunctions**
are joining words.

8 **Interjections**
show emotion, feeling
or a reaction.

Here's a hoary old rhyme to help you remember them:

Every name is called a Noun as field and fountain, street and town.

In place of a noun the Pronoun stands, as he and she clap their hands.

The Adjective describes a thing, as magic wand or bridal ring.

The Verb means action, something done, to read and write, to jump and run.

How things are done, the Adverb tells, as quickly, slowly, badly, well.

The Preposition shows relation, as in the street or at the station.

The Conjunction joins in many ways, sentences, words or phrase and phrase.

The Interjection cries out 'Hark! I need an exclamation mark!'

Often confused

censor: suppress unacceptable parts of a work (book, film, etc.)

censure: (v) express severe disapproval of; (n) expression of severe disapproval

disinterested: (adj) impartial, not influenced by considerations of personal gain

uninterested: (adj) having or feeling no interest in something

bear: (v) carry, take responsibility for; (v) give birth; (v) turn in a specific direction; (n) large, heavy ursine mammal

bare: (adj) not clothed or covered, devoid of; (v) expose a part of the body to view

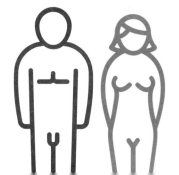

Ten reasons to use an apostrophe

There are only <u>ten reasons</u> for using an <u>apostrophe</u>. Whether you are compiling a business report or scribbling the specials on a pub chalkboard, these same simple rules apply.

Rule 1

**Use the apostrophe
with** contractions**.
The apostrophe always
replaces the missing letter.**

Do not   Don't

Is not   Isn't

He has arrived.   He's arrived.

Rule 2

Use the apostrophe to show
possession **– that something
belongs to someone.**

The woman's coat

The man's umbrella

The cat's whiskers

The bishop's finger

Tames's house

Rule 3

**Use the apostrophe when the noun
is** implied**.**

'This is your carrot. This is my horse's.

Rule 4

When using <u>plural possession</u>, make the plural first and then place the apostrophe after it.

The apples' flavour was bitter.

The three windows' light

The flavour of the apples was bitter. (no apostrophes, because no possession)

The light from three windows (no apostrophes, because no possession)

Rule 5

Don't use the apostrophe for the plural of a name.

They mentioned the Browns on the news.

The Johnsons attended the wedding.

Rule 6

If two or more people <u>possess the same thing,</u> only use apostrophe 's' after the second person.

Jack and Jill's bucket

Phil and Graham's wedding

Rule 7

Nobody would think of using an apostrophe with the word 'mine', but lots of people get confused by the 's' in other possessive pronouns like his, hers, its, theirs, ours, yours and whose. <u>No apostrophe is required here</u> even though it is possessive.

This bowl is yours.

That tree has a ball wedged in its branches.

Whose wallet is this? It is not theirs.

Rule 8

<u>Only ever</u> use 'it's' for a <u>contraction</u> of 'it is' or 'it has'.

It's cloudy today.

It's been cloudy today.

Rule 9

The plurals for capitals or numbers used as nouns do not use apostrophes.

I have just sat my SATs.
(not SAT's)

That was normal during the 1980s.
(not 1980's)

Nobody buys DVDs any more.
(not DVD's)

Rule 10

The apostrophe goes after the thing doing the possessing.

the moon's reflection
(the reflection of the moon)

a week's pay
(the pay of a week)

two weeks' pay
(the pay of two weeks)

everyone's choice
(the choice of everyone)

Finally, in most cases, phrases such as 'girls school', 'Fathers Day', 'visitors book' and 'workers canteen' should not include apostrophes because there is no possession involved.

girls school: a school for girls,
not owned by girls

visitors book: a book for visitors,
not owned by visitors

However, there are a few exceptions such as All Saints' Day and All Souls' Day, which do have an apostrophe even though they're not owned by saints/souls.

<u>Common</u> <u>grammar</u> <u>mistakes</u>

Their/They're /There

'<u>Their</u>' is only used to indicate possession – something that belongs to 'them'.

'<u>They're</u>' is only used as a contraction of 'they are'.

'<u>There</u>' is used for everywhere else, either to refer to a place that is 'over there' or to make a statement, e.g. 'There is no bread left.'

Figures of speech

Paraprosdokian

From the Greek para meaning 'contrary to' and prosdokia meaning 'expectation', it occurs when a surprising twist ending forces the reader or listener to reinterpret the first part of a sentence or passage of writing. This comic technique is also known as 'pull back and reveal'.

Often confused

oral: (adj) spoken rather than written; relating to the mouth

aural: (adj) heard; relating to the ear or hearing

stationery: (n) writing and other office materials [remember: an envelope is stationery]

stationary: (adj) not moving

adverse: (adj) preventing success or development

averse: (adj) having a strong dislike of or opposition to something

Writing tips

Use the active voice

One of the best pieces of writing advice you'll ever learn is 'Use the active voice'. In other words, make sure that the person, animal or thing that is connected to the verb <u>does the doing!</u>

Figure out the verb in the sentence and then make the subject drive the verb.

'Jane threw the ball' is active voice.

'The ball was thrown by Jane' is passive voice.

'The banquet was enjoyed by everyone.' This is passive voice. **'Everyone enjoyed the banquet' is more direct and immediate, simpler and easier to read, and altogether more satisfying, because it is** active voice.

Also, in the sentence at the top of the page, '... you'll ever learn' is active, **'... you'll ever be taught' would be** passive.

Paraprosdokian

Marriage is a great
institution, but I'm not ready
for an institution.
Mae West

Often confused

due to: caused by

owing to: because of

elude: (v) escape from, avoid

allude: (v) suggest or call attention to indirectly

farther: by a greater (physical) distance

further: by a greater (metaphorical) distance

Common grammar mistakes

Could/would /should of

Could/would/should followed by '**of**' is **always wrong**. Never use it. The reason this error has become so common in speech is that the correct contraction of 'should have' – which is 'should've' – sounds a bit like 'should of'.

Correct	Correct	Always wrong
could have	could've	could of
would have	would've	would of
should have	should've	should of

Order of
Adjectives

Native English speakers know instinctively how to arrange their adjectives before a noun just because 'it sounds right', but there's a rule for that! When describing something with more than one adjective, you should arrange them in order of number, opinion, size, age, shape, color, origin, material, purpose and proper adjective (an adjective formed from a proper noun and spelled with an initial capital letter, e.g. Shakespearean).

Whimperative

This portmanteau word blend of whimper + imperative was coined by theoretical linguist Jerrold Sadock in 1970. It is the conversational convention of disguising an order (imperative statement) as a question to turn it into a polite request. For example, the abruptness of 'Pass the salt, please' sounds rude, so a polite speaker would customarily change such a request into a question – the whimperative – so it becomes 'Could you pass the salt, please?'

Paraprosdokian

A bank is a place
that will lend you
money, if you can
prove that you don't
need it.
Bob Hope

Figures of speech

Oxymoron

Two contradictory ideas
placed in the same sentence,
for example:

<u>deafening</u> silence
<u>deeply</u> superficial
<u>painfully</u> beautiful
<u>passive</u> aggressive
<u>keenly</u> stupid

Collective nouns
Singular or plural verbs?

Collective nouns are nouns that stand for a group or collection of people or things. They include words such as army, audience, board, class, community, crew, crowd, family, group, panel, staff, team and troupe.

In American English, most collective nouns are paired with a singular verb:

The whole family was watching television.

The panel is making its decision.

The team is giving one of its finest performances.

In British English, most collective nouns can be singular or plural:

The whole family was/were watching television.

The panel is/are making its/their decision.

The team is/are giving one of its/their finest performances.

There are a few collective nouns (in both British and American English) that are always used with either a singular or plural verb, for example, 'community' and most animal collective nouns like 'herd', 'flock', 'pack' and 'litter' are always singular, and 'people' and 'police' are always plural.

The community is devastated by this tragedy.

The herd was decimated by the attack.

People are often prepared to listen.

The police have been more visible in the area.

Often confused

---

breach: **(v) (n) break**

breech: **(v) bottom first (of a birth); (n) the back part of a rifle or gun barrel**

---

broach: **(v) raise (a difficult subject) for discussion; to pierce a container to draw out liquid**

brooch: **(n) an ornament fastened to clothing with a hinged pin and catch**

---

canvass: **(v) solicit votes; propose an idea**

canvas: **(n) strong, coarse unbleached cloth used to make sails and tents and as a surface for oil painting**

Common grammar mistakes

Missing comma after introductory component

You should always use a comma after an introductory word, phrase or clause, this allows the reader to pause and avoids the confusion of it qualifying the rest of the sentence.

Incorrect: The first time we met I felt certain we would become good friends.

Correct: The first time we met, I felt certain we would become good friends.

If the introductory component is a 'restrictive appositive phrase' (a sort of compound subject), don't use a comma to separate it from the main clause.

Incorrect: The American swimmer, Michael Phelps, won twenty-three Olympic gold medals.

Correct: The American swimmer Michael Phelps won twenty-three Olympic gold medals.

Paraprosdokian

Always borrow money
from a pessimist. He won't
expect it back.
Oscar Wilde

A myriad of
Myriad/myriads

Most linguists agree that either is acceptable. The word 'myriad' began life as a noun that literally meant 'ten thousand', so back then, adding 'of' would have been wrong. Today, the word is both a noun and an adjective.

myriad [innumerable] = adjective

a myriad/myriads [variety/varieties, large unspecified number/s] of
= noun

Ending sentences with prepositions

It's not wrong if it sounds right ...

The bogus rule about avoiding ending a sentence with a preposition (which linguists call 'preposition stranding') was introduced by the poet and playwright John Dryden in 1672, in objection to Ben Jonson's phrase 'the bodies that those souls were frighted from'. This was probably because it's not allowed in Latin, and we've been stuck with it ever since.

In great literature, there are plenty of perfectly acceptable examples that read fluently. Geoffrey Chaucer, John Milton and William Shakespeare all blithely stranded prepositions prior to Dryden, and many great authors since have broken this so-called 'rule'. Jane Austen wrote 'Fanny could with difficulty give the smile that was asked for'; James Joyce penned 'He had enough money to settle down on' and the famous admonition, 'This is the sort of tedious nonsense up with which I will not put' has been apocryphally attributed to Winston Churchill.

Here are four examples of perfectly acceptable sentences that end with a preposition:

The food had not even been accounted for.

The baseball game was rained off.

What did you do that for?

I hope you know just what you're taking on.

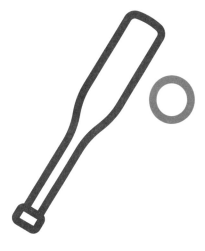

Often confused

fewer: not as many

less: not as much

If you can count the things being described (cakes, opportunities, coins, horses, buttons, people, countries, pieces), use 'fewer'; if you can't count the things (cake, opportunity, money, hope, music, sunshine), use 'less'.

diffuse: (n) (adj) spread out over a large area

defuse: (v) remove the fuse; make less dangerous

fortunate: (adj) involving good luck; lucky

fortuitous: (adj) happening by (lucky) chance rather than intention

Common grammar mistakes

Dangling participles

A dangling participle is a common example of a misplaced modifier often caused when the writer begins a sentence with a participle that doesn't refer to the subject of the sentence.

Climbing to the summit, my lungs started to feel sore.

Here, the phrase 'my lungs' has incorrectly become the subject of the verb 'climbing', so the sentence needs rewording to remove the dangling participle:

As I was climbing to the summit, my lungs started to feel sore.

Climbing to the summit, I found that my lungs started to feel sore.

Paraprosdokian

I've had a perfectly wonderful evening.
But this wasn't it.
Hugh Herbert

She told him that she
Loved him

It is possible to make eight sentences with more than eight different meanings simply by adding the word 'only'.

1. **Only she told him that she loved him.**
   Nobody else told him.

2. **She only told him that she loved him.**
   What's the big deal? She didn't tell him anything else.

3. **She told only him that she loved him.**
   She told nobody else, only him.

4. **She told him only that she loved him.**
   She didn't tell him anything else.

5. **She told him that only she loved him.**
   Nobody else loved him except her.

6. **She told him that she only loved him.**
   She loved him and him alone.
   All she did was love him.

7. **She told him that she loved only him.**
   She loved him and him alone.

8. **She told him that she loved him only.**
   He was the only one she loved.

E.g. and i.e.

Both are Latin abbreviations, but they aren't interchangeable. This is how and when to use them:

e.g. is from the Latin <u>exempli gratia</u> **(for example). It is used before giving an example. For example:**

This behaviour can be explained by Newton's first law of motion, e.g. the red ball remained at rest because there was no external force acting on it.

---

i.e. is from the Latin <u>id est</u> **(that is). It is used before offering further clarification. For example:**

This behaviour can be explained by Newton's first law of motion, i.e. every object will remain at rest or in uniform motion in a straight line unless compelled to change its state by the action of an external force.

Figures of speech
Hyperbole

The use of exaggeration, usually not meant to be taken literally, for example:

I've told you a million times.

I am giving 110 per cent.

I am so hungry I could eat a horse.

Rhetorical devices
Anaphora

Repeating a word or phrase at the beginning of neighbouring clauses, lending them emphasis – for example:

I have a dream that one day this nation will rise up ... I have a dream that one day on the red hills of Georgia ... I have a dream that my four little children ... I have a dream that one day in Alabama ... I have a dream today ... I have a dream that one day every valley shall be exalted ...

Martin Luther King, Jr.

Paraprosdokian

To steal ideas from one
person is plagiarism.
To steal from many is
research.
Anon.

Often confused

titillate: (v) arouse (someone) to interest or excitement, especially through sexually suggestive images or words

titivate: (v) make minor enhancements; smarten up

tortuous: (adj) full of twists and turns; excessively lengthy and complicated

torturous: (adj) characterised by, involving or causing pain or suffering

wreath: (n) decorative ring-shaped arrangement typically of flora, often for laying on a grave

wreathe: (v) cover, surround or encircle

Common grammar mistakes

Misplaced or dangling modifier

A misplaced modifier is a word, phrase or clause that is separated incorrectly from the word it modifies or describes, often with hilarious results. Many jokes rely on a misplaced modifier in the setup, which is revealed by the punch line, like in this old classic by Groucho Marx:

'One morning I shot an elephant in my pajamas. How he got into my pajamas I'll never know.'

To avoid confusion (and ruin the joke), say, 'One morning, while wearing my pajamas, I shot an elephant.'

When to use
Ellipses

An ellipsis (plural ellipses) is three full stops used to show that some words have been omitted from a piece of text, often a quotation:

'The quality of mercy … droppeth as the gentle rain from heaven … twice blest.'

It is also used in dialogue to show that the speaker trails off:
'But I thought you said …'

It can be used to demonstrate the continuation of a sequence:
2, 4, 8, 16, 32 …

Some editors put a letter space on either or both sides of the ellipsis; others leave no spaces. So long as you are consistent within a piece of work, choose whichever feels the most comfortable.

Often confused

affect: (v) have an effect on; make a difference to; move emotionally

effect: (n) result or consequence of an action; the state of being or becoming operative ('with effect from tomorrow')

advice: (n) guidance or recommendations offered with regard to favorable action

advise: (v) offer guidance or recommendations

prevaricate: (v) lie, deceive, act in an evasive way

procrastinate: (v) delay or postpone action

Figures of speech
Metonymy

To substitute one word or phrase for another with which it is closely associated, for example:

'crown' for 'royalty'

'The White House' for 'The Administration/President'

'Hollywood' for 'the American film industry'

Paraprosdokian

If I said you had a beautiful body,
would you hold it against me?
David Bellamy

Half – singular or plural?

The answer is – both!

Half on its own is always singular:
My half is stale.

It is also singular when it modifies a singular:
My half of the pizza is stale.

It is plural when it modifies a plural:
My half of the pizzas are stale.

When to capitalize sun/earth/moon

The other celestial bodies, such as Mars, Mercury and Jupiter are always capitalized, but the capitalization of sun, earth and moon depends on context.

Usually, you <u>don't</u> have to capitalize earth, sun and moon:

The sun is shining this morning. The moon was bright last night. The earth continues to rotate on its axis. I like living here on earth.

However, you must capitalize when they are mentioned in the context of other celestial bodies which are capitalized:

Mercury is the smallest planet – it is only slightly larger than Earth's moon.

Mercury is the smallest planet – it is only slightly larger than our Moon.

Common grammar mistakes

Colon use after a phrase

Only use a colon in a sentence if the preceding words could form a standalone sentence.
For example:

Error: My friend asked me to buy: fruit, bread, milk and washing powder.

Correction: My friend asked me to buy some supplies: fruit, bread, milk and washing powder.

Often confused

hanged: executed by hanging

hung: attached to a hook on a wall

looser: (adj) less tight

loser: (n) a person or thing that loses

older: (adj) having lived for a longer time

elder: (adj) (of one or more out of a group of associated people) of a greater age; (n) person who is older

Figures of speech

Synecdoche

A specific type of metonymy in which a phrase is replaced with an associated phrase, but where a part replaces a whole, or a whole replaces a part – for example:

'wheels' **for** 'car'

'skirt' **for** 'woman'

'suit' **for** 'office worker'

'sails' **for** 'ships'

'glass' **for** 'glass of wine'

Paraprosdokian

I used to be indecisive.
Now I'm not sure ...
Tommy Cooper

When to use
Initial capital letters

Initial capital letters (uppercase first letter of a word) are often misused, especially on signage and when used for emphasis. There are only ten basic uses for an initial capital. If it doesn't appear here, and you're in doubt, use lowercase instead.

1. First word of a sentence or line of poetry

2. Proper noun (name used for an individual person, place, organization, movement): Jane, New York, Walmart, the President, Buddhism, Islam

3. For major words in the titles of books, plays, films, works of art, organizations: The God of Small Things, One Flew Over the Cuckoo's Nest, Girl with a Pearl Earring, Washington Chamber of Commerce (but lowercase when referring to a general one, e.g. 'I visited the local chamber of commerce.')

4. Proper names of periods of time, historical eras and events: Palaeozoic Era, Bronze Age, Classical, Renaissance, Middle Ages, First World War

5. For abbreviations and acronyms: NBC, ATM, USAF

6. For adjectives derived from proper nouns: Shakespearean, American, Bostonian

7. For the pronoun 'I'

8. For personal titles that are linked to a name: Mr, Mrs, Dr, Reverend, King Louis, Sir, Bishop of Oxford (but lowercase when more general: 'He consulted the bishop.')

9. Days of the week, months of the year and special occasions: Easter Sunday, Christmas Day, World Book Day

10. Brand names: Mercedes, Amazon, Nike

Double negatives

A double negative uses two negative words incorrectly in the same clause to express a single negative idea.
For example:

We didn't do nothing/nuffin.
[= We did nothing.]

He never spoke with nobody. [= He didn't speak with anybody.]

Double negatives are acceptable in many other languages, and they were standard in English during the Middle Ages, However, today, although the meaning of a double negative is clear, using one in speech is clumsy and lacks sophistication.

There is only one type of double negative that is grammatically correct:

As a classical actor, he was not unfamiliar with the plays of Shakespeare.

While I am not unconvinced by his sincerity …

This subtle use of the double negative expresses a small amount of doubt and even ironic understatement, which is known as litotes – stating a negative to further affirm a positive.

Often confused

cue: (n) a signal for action; (v) give a signal for action; (n) tapering wooden rod used in snooker and billiards

queue: (n) a line or sequence of people or vehicles awaiting their turn; (v) participate in such a line

reactionary: (adj) opposing political or social progress or reform; (n) a reactionary person

revolutionary: (adj) involving or causing a complete or dramatic change; (n) a person who advocates or engages in political revolution

learnt: (v) gained by study or by being taught

learned: (adj) having acquired much knowledge through study

<u>Figures of speech</u>

Enallage

To give a sentence improper grammar **intentionally by replacing one grammatical form (person, case, gender, number, tense) by another that is ungrammatical, to make it more** memorable **– for example:**

'If it ain't broke, don't fix it.'

'You pays your money, and you takes your chances.'

'We was robbed!'

'Thanking you'

'Exsqueeze me'

'Think different'
(Apple Computer, Inc. 1997)

Paraprosdokian

I didn't say it was your fault;
I said I was blaming you.
Anon.

Rhetorical devices

Epistrophe

Repeating a word or phrase at the end of neighbouring clauses, lending them emphasis, for example:

When I was a child, I spoke as a child, I understood as a child, I thought as a child; but when I became a man, I put away childish things.
1 Corinthians 13:11

What is the
Subjunctive?

The subjunctive is one of three moods (the other two are indicative and imperative).

Indicative: the verb makes a statement or asks a question: 'James cooks once a week' or 'Does James cook once a week?'

Imperative: the verb expresses direct commands, prohibitions and requests: 'Cook for me, right now', 'Stop cooking immediately' or 'Please cook me a meal'.

Subjunctive: the verb stem is used to express wishes and hypothetical suggestions:

'If only I could see him one more time.'

'I suggest that you drive more carefully.'

'How about I do the washing up this evening?'

'She demanded that he leave the building.'

Paraprosdokian

I used to do drugs. I still do,
but I used to, too.
Mitch Hedberg

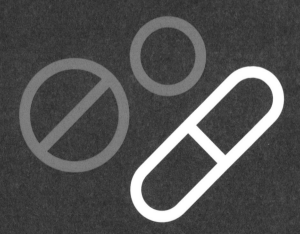

Often confused

forbear: (v) restrain an impulse to do something; refrain

forebear: (n) ancestor

grisly: (adj) causing horror or disgust

grizzly: (n) large brown bear

hoard: (n) a stock or store of money or valued objects; (v) accumulate

horde: (n) a large group of people; army of nomadic warriors

I never said she stole

my money

In English grammar as in life, stress is important!
This sentence has seven different meanings
depending on which word you stress:

---

1. **I never said she stole my money.**
   Someone else did.

---

2. **I never said she stole my money.**
   I would never do such a thing.

---

3. **I never said she stole my money.**
   I may have implied it, or written it down, or pointed at
   her, but I never actually said she stole my money.

---

4. **I never said she stole my money.**
   I said someone stole it, but I didn't single her out.

---

5. **I never said she stole my money.**
   I said she borrowed it, ate it, wasted it, hid it … she
   definitely did something with it.

---

6. **I never said she stole my money.**
   She is the thief, but it wasn't my money that she stole.

---

7. **I never said she stole my money.**
   She stole something from me, but it wasn't my money.

Common grammar mistakes

Split infinitives

An infinitive is the word 'to' with a verb. A split infinitive occurs when another word (often an adverb) separates the word 'to' and the verb.

The world's most famous split infinitive appeared at the beginning of every episode of the original Star Trek television series: 'To boldly go where no man has gone before!' The adverb 'boldly' splits 'to' from the infinitive 'go'. However, since there is no grammar rule explicitly forbidding split infinitives, they aren't wrong but they can often sound clumsy.

What is a

Hypocorism?

A hypocorism is the diminutive form of a name, a pet name, nickname, etc. (e.g. Tom or Tommy for Thomas, Al or Ally for Alison, Peggy for Margaret, Hank for Henry), but it also refers to the use of forms of speech imitative of baby talk, especially by an adult ('doggy', 'moo-cow', 'Nana' for Grandma, 'num-num' for baby's dummy).

Figures of speech

Zeugma

In Greek, <u>zeugma</u> means 'a yoking'. As a figure of speech, it refers to where a single word or phrase is used to modify and link two words with different meanings. For example:

I lost my keys and my temper.

'Yet time and her aunt moved slowly.'
Jane Austen, <u>Pride and Prejudice</u>

'Yes, my teeth and ambitions are bared.'
Scar, <u>The Lion King</u>

Often confused

forward: (adv) in the direction that one is facing or travelling

foreword: (n) a short introduction to a book

accept: (v) consent to receive or undertake (something offered)

except: (v) exclude from a category or group; (prep) not including; (conj) excluding (to show something is not part of what has been stated before)

aloud: (adv) audibly, not silently

allowed: (v) (adj) permitted

Often confused

currant: (n) small dried seedless grape

current: (adj) belonging to the present time; (n) flow of electricity, water or air

discreet: (adj) careful and prudent in one's speech or actions

discrete: (adj) individually separate and distinct

flounder: (v) struggle clumsily in mud or water; show great confusion

founder: (v) to fill with water and sink; (n) caster of metal; a person who establishes an institution or settlement

Paraprosdokian

I'm against picketing, but I
don't know how to show it.
Mitch Hedberg

Two dashes and a hyphen

Em-dash/en-dash/hyphen

They are **not** interchangeable!

Em-dash

The unspaced em-dash is still used in American English instead of parentheses, but in Standard English, the spaced en-dash is now more commonly used in this context. The only time you'd use the unspaced em-dash nowadays would be in dialogue when the speaker is interrupted mid-word or sentence:

'I love you—'
'Don't say that.'

or

'I love y—'
'Please don't.'

En-dash

The en-dash has several uses. It appears spaced for parentheses, as discussed above. It is also used to connect two words, where the first part of a compound word does not modify the meaning of the second:

'The North–South divide', 'the Klitschko–Fury title fight' and 'the Watson–Crick structure of DNA' use an unspaced en-dash but 'north-west' and 'blue-green' use hyphens.

Also use an en-dash with multiple compounds, e.g:
'He wears jam jar–bottom glasses' and 'The album included new age–style music' because 'bottom' and 'style' are connected to 'jam jar' and 'new age' not just 'jar' and 'age'.

Use an en-dash (not a hyphen) between numbers:

The 2017–2018 season
11:00am–1:00pm

There are lots of other obscure examples of dash usage, but for everyday purposes, you can use a hyphen safely everywhere else (usually in compound words).

Hyphen

Anything with 'self' followed by a noun or adjective, needs a hyphen (self-esteem, self-assembly, self-conscious).

'xx century' uses a hyphen only when qualifying a noun, so 'in the eighteenth century' and 'eighteenth-century clothing' are correct.

'I hate being told-off', 'please mop-up this mess' and 'finish-off this assignment' all use the hyphen incorrectly. No hyphen is needed because 'told', 'mop' and 'finish' are all being used as verbs and not adjectives.

Paraprosdokian

Where there's a will, I want
to be in it.
Anon.

Common grammar mistakes
Subject–verb agreement

The subject and verb of a sentence must agree with each other in number.

For example:

Error: **Most of my friends likes to eat Chinese food.**
Correction: **Most of my friends like to eat Chinese food.**

When you have a list of subjects, the verb is plural except when the subjects are linked as a unit.

France, Spain and Italy have many football supporters. [plural verb '**have**']

Charlie and the Chocolate Factory is a popular book. [singular verb '**is**' because Charlie and the Chocolate Factory is a unit]

Often confused

coarse: (adj) rough or harsh in texture

course: (n) the route or direction followed by something; series of lessons; dish as part of a meal

complement: (n) a thing that helps to improve something else; a number or quantity that completes a group

compliment: (n) polite expression of praise or admiration; (v) to express praise or admiration

council: (n) an administrative/advisory body of people

counsel: (n) advice, especially that given formally; (v) to give advice

Fun with
Morphology

An **inchoative verb** (aka an 'inceptive verb') expresses the **beginning** of an action. You can turn some adjectives into inchoative verbs, simply by adding the affix 'en':

stiff	→ stiffen		**dark**	→ darken
smart	→ smarten		**red**	→ redden
hard	→ harden		**tough**	→ toughen
fresh	→ freshen		**bright**	→ brighten
quick	→ quicken		**broad**	→ broaden

But most adjectives **don't** work like this – for example: gold, small, orange, dry, happy, gentle, delightful.

Cannot or can not?

Both 'cannot' and 'can not' are permissible **spellings, but the first is more commonly used. You would have to use 'can not' when the 'not' is part of another phrase such as 'not only'.**

For example:

These all-rounders can not only bat, they can bowl adequately too.

Can or may?

When you ask for permission, which word should you use – 'can' or 'may'?

Grammatically you can use either, although 'may' is considered more polite and respectful.

'Can I take your coat?'
'May I take your coat?'

'Can I take the rest of the day off?'
'May I take the rest of the day off?'

'Can I borrow this newspaper?'
'May I borrow this newspaper?'

Recently, the phrase 'Can I get?' has crept into the English language, and is commonly used by people under the age of 30 when ordering food or drink. Critics argue that it sounds rude, acquisitive and entitled, but users prefer its directness. Since it is still a whimperative construction (see page 21), we are still a long way from 'I'll have …' or 'Get me …'.

Paraprosdokian

If everything seems under control, you're just not going fast enough.
Mario Andretti

Figures of speech

Homeric epithet

Homeric epithets are phrases that are repeatedly associated with – or replace – a noun.

They formed a large repertoire of stock ready-made language units that could be fitted into the dactylic hexameter (six metrical units – feet – in each line) used in Homer's <u>Iliad</u> and <u>Odyssey</u>: grey-eyed Athena, cloud-gathering Zeus, wise Penelope, rosy-fingered dawn, wine-dark sea, sensible Telemachus, swift-footed Achilles, son of Peleus (= Achilles). Today, the world-popular oral tradition of rap music has a similar repertoire of stock phrases such as 'to the beat', 'bust a cap', 'fo shizzle', 'kickin' it', 'oh fo sure', 'sticky icky', 'Maybelline', 'chronic', etc.

Common grammar mistakes

Vague pronoun reference

A **pronoun** can replace a **noun**. However, try to avoid another noun creeping in between the pronoun and the noun it replaces, otherwise the reader won't know which noun the pronoun has replaced. The pronoun and noun must also agree in person, number and gender. For example:

Error: When Kate finally found her cat, she was filthy. (Kate or the cat?)

Correction: Kate finally found her filthy cat.

Different from, than or to?

The phrases 'different from', 'different than' and 'different to' are broadly interchangeable and mean the same thing. The most common of the three is undoubtedly 'different from'. UK English speakers also use 'different to' whereas 'different than' is more common in American English.

Bullet points

Bullet points are used to **draw attention** to (and often to summarize) **important information**.

They can be used quite flexibly, but there are a few general rules. The text introducing the bullet point list should end in a colon, but the bullet points don't have to complete the sentence or even form a sentence – they can be single word or phrases. If they are complete sentences, they should start with a capital letter and end with a full stop, otherwise no commas or full stops are required. Finally, it is advisable to begin each bullet point with the same part of speech (verb, noun, etc.) for simplicity and greater impact.

Often confused

imply: (v) indicate the truth or existence of (something) by suggestion

infer: (v) deduce or conclude (something) from evidence and reasoning

loath: (adj) reluctant; unwilling

loathe: (v) feel intense dislike or disgust for; hate

Often confused

assent: (v) express approval or agreement; (n) the expression of approval or agreement

ascent: (n) an upward climb or walk (to a summit)

born: (adj) given birth to

borne: (adj) carried

bourn: (n) small stream; boundary, limit; goal

chord: (n) group of three or more notes sounded together

cord: (n) thin, flexible string or rope made from twisted strands

Paraprosdokian

War does not determine who is right –
only who is left.
Bertrand Russell

Figures of speech

Hendiatris
(aka the rule of three)

Used for emphasis, in which three words are used to express one idea – for example:

'I came, I saw, I conquered.'

sex, drugs and rock 'n' roll

wine, women and song

Liberty, Equality, Fraternity

Snap! Crackle! Pop!

Missing comma after introductory element

Always use a comma <u>after</u> an introductory word, phrase or clause. For example:

Error: At six o'clock he rang the bell for supper.

Correction: At six o'clock, he rang the bell for supper.

Rhetorical devices

Chiasmus

From the Greek for 'diagonal arrangement', chiasmus refers to where two or more key elements are repeated but in reverse order, to produce a clever turn of phrase.

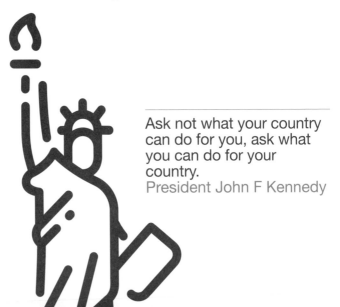

Ask not what your country can do for you, ask what you can do for your country.
President John F Kennedy

When the going gets tough, the tough get going!

All for one, and one for all.

You can take the boy out of the country, but you can't take the country out of the boy.

I'd rather have a bottle in front of me, than a frontal lobotomy.
Dorothy Parker

It's not the men in my life, it's the life in my men.
Mae West

I have taken more out of alcohol than alcohol has taken out of me.
Winston Churchill

Often confused

prescribe: (v) stipulate, lay down the law; authorize the use of medicine for someone

proscribe: (v) forbid, especially by law; denounce, condemn

principal: (adj) first in order of importance; (n) head of an organization, especially a school; lead performer

principle: (n) fundamental truth or proposition that supports a system of belief or behaviour

storey: (n) a single level of a building

story: (n) fictional account; plot or storyline

Paraprosdokian

The difference between stupidity and
genius is that genius has its limits.
Albert Einstein

What is illeism?

Referring to oneself using the third person instead of the first person is called illeism, a term coined by Samuel Taylor Coleridge in 1809. Today, it is considered narcissistic and displays a certain detachment from reality. Here are some examples of famous illeists:

Julius Caesar: Fictional accounts such as Shakespeare's play <u>Julius Caesar</u> and the comic-strip series <u>Asterix the Gaul</u> portray him correctly as an illeist – he frequently used illeism in his own historical writings.

Caesar should be a beast without a heart
If he should stay at home today for fear.
No, Caesar shall not. Danger knows full well
That Caesar is more dangerous than he.
Julius Caesar, Act II, Scene II

You won't have Nixon to kick around
anymore, because, gentlemen, this is my
last press conference.
Richard Nixon

Can you smell what The Rock is cooking?
The Rock (Dwayne Johnson, during his
wrestling days)

Terry loves yogurt.
Terry Jeffords (Terry Crews, Brooklyn
Nine-Nine)

**Other famous illeists include
Flavor Flav, LeBron James, Jimmy
from Seinfeld and Donald Trump.**

**Queen Victoria is believed to have
uttered the notorious phrase 'We
are not amused' to rebuke a ribald
dinner guest at Windsor Castle.
However, there is no hard evidence,
and she may well have been
speaking on behalf of all the women
present, rather than using illeism.**

Paraprosdokian

Change is inevitable, except from a vending machine.
Robert Gallagher

Often confused

ensure: (v) make certain that (something) will occur or be the case

insure: (v) arrange for compensation in the event of damage, loss or injury

flaunt: (v) display (something) ostentatiously, usually to provoke a response

flout: (v) openly disregard (a rule, law or convention)

Figures of speech

Transferred epithet

A **transferred epithet** is a little-known – but often used – figure of speech where a modifier (usually an adjective) qualifies a noun <u>other</u> than the object or person it is describing – for example:

wonderful day	unhappy marriage
sleepless night	angry finger
careless whisper	cheeky pint
disabled toilet	

Rhetorical devices

Antanaclasis

Repetition of a single **word** or phrase, with **two** **different meanings** – **for example:**

Time flies like an arrow; fruit flies like a banana.

We must all hang together, or assuredly we shall all hang separately.
Ben Franklin

Common grammar mistakes

Vague pronoun reference

When you are referring to yourself and another person, if you are unsure whether to use 'I' or 'me', remove the other person from the sentence and see what makes sense.

For example, in the sentence 'Me and James went fishing', removing 'James' leaves the incorrect sentence 'Me went fishing', so 'James and I went fishing' must be correct. You wouldn't say, 'I and James went fishing' because it just sounds wrong, although you might say 'I and several others went fishing'. Sometimes you just have to use your ear and some common sense.

People overuse 'myself', especially when they are trying to be polite or formal. Only use 'myself' in these three circumstances:

as the object of a verb ('I tried to calm myself.') – 'me' would sound wrong here

as the object of a preposition ('I prefer to be by myself.')

to add emphasis ('I chose it myself';
'I myself find the idea repulsive.').

The most common incorrect use of 'myself' is in place of 'I' or 'me', especially where there are two or more people. For example, 'Please could you book a reservation for my business partner and myself' sounds superficially more polite and sophisticated than the correct sentence, 'Please could you book a reservation for my business partner and me', but it is wrong and makes the speaker sound clumsy and ill-educated.

Common grammar mistakes

Sentence fragments

Sentence fragments are incomplete sentences that lack an essential element such as a subject or a complete verb, and often rely on the preceding sentence for their meaning. They have a useful purpose in poetry or narrative fiction, but they are best avoided in formal prose. For example:

Error: He stroked the dog and let it lick him. In spite of his fear.

Correction: He stroked the dog and let it lick him, in spite of his fear.